AF668111

ENTER TO PRENEUR

Change your Interest to Business

BY MAHA VIGNESH N

Copyright © 2022 by Maha Vignesh N

All rights reserved.

No portion of this book may be reproduced in any form without written permission from the publisher or author, except as permitted by U.S. copyright law.

ISBN: 978-93-5779-791-7

Dedication

I dedicate this book to every ordinary young person striving for success. To every parent who motivates their children to succeed. To every life destroyer who creates new age leaders by shaming, disrespecting, and destroying lives.

Acknowledgements

Don't be afraid to express your appreciation at any time. I am grateful to my parents for shaping me in this way. I am grateful to my life's teachers, mentors, and gurus for pointing me in the right direction. Special thanks to Nancy D Dhanya for giving me the confidence to write this book. I'd like to thank my entire team for being here with me. Finally, I appreciate your interest in reading this book.

Content

WHY should you READ this BOOK?

Everyone in this world only believes in the real. We expect the impossible, but we believe in reality.

Do you want to know the sexiest way to succeed wisely? Do you have trouble determining your area of interest? Are you concerned about money while you're learning? Are you looking for a way to transition from normal to successful? My friend, this is the book for you.

My name is Maha Vignesh, and I am the son of Muneeswari, Nagarajan. I own 3 profitable and innovative businesses. We built this meaningful life after going through the most difficult times. My parents began their lives in a lower-class environment. They worked their way up to the upper-middle class. They provided me with a good education, life lessons, and a good way of life. I am the one in majority of people in the world. The vast majority of people desire success but are unsure of how to achieve it. Perhaps you are among the majority. The problems and financial difficulties that my family and I have faced are indescribable. We've met a lot of bad people in our lives. I was destroyed like the majority of people, but I fought back like the successful people. So, my life lessons will undoubtedly provide you with a different perspective on achieving success. *Provide you with an earning strategy while you are still in the learning stage.*

I went through various stages of my life to get to this point. I divided my life into three sections. By following the three phases of discovery, learning, and mindset. Three stages led me to this point. As I previously stated, I am a normal being with many pains, barriers, struggles, betrayals, distractions, and a poor mentality who has overcome all of life's brutality. With my life, I made a peace after a war. I discovered the wise and genuine path to success in life by starting a business or working. I belong to the vast majority of people on the planet. So, I decided to show the way to everyone else in the world who is struggling like me.

PHASE 1 FINDING

1
PAHSE FINDING

Welcome to the first phase of your journey. I am grateful to have you along for the journey. During this phase, we will discover our areas of interest. What exactly does the term "interest" mean? How to Pick a Passion How to expand our knowledge of our passion. At the end of this first phase, you will have a clear idea of what you want to do with your life. So, are you prepared? Welcome to PHASE 1!

1.1. Find Interest

What makes you unique? What makes you unique in a group of people? Think for a moment. You are in your college, and numerous sessions are in progress. But during one session, you are at the height of your enthusiasm, correct? Why are you really behaving that way?

Consider another circumstance. You were at the park when you unintentionally ran into someone you know well. Why would you leave for the height of surprise?

Once more, another circumstance. You checked into your preferred hotel, but your preferred cuisine was out of stock. You'll feel so upset that you'll consider having lunch at a different hotel, and occasionally you'll skip lunch. Why?

Why? Why? Why do you respond that way in different circumstances? Take a comprehensive look at all the possibilities. You might have been so engaged in that particular lesson because you were so knowledgeable about the subject or because the lecturer was your crush. Haha, I'm kidding. However, something you might know about that lecturer if you had a crush on him or her. We cannot fall in love with someone just because we want to or based solely on how they look. You are drawn to one of that person's distinctive qualities, which indicates that you are aware of that person's most alluring quality and have a crush on them for that reason. You have an interest in someone because you know them extremely well—that is, you are familiar with their nature, character, lifestyle, finances, favourite meal, location, song, actor, and movie, among other things. As a result, that person has become quite close to you. Consequently, you got very excited when you unexpectedly ran into that person. In a restaurant setting, you sampled the cuisine, so you know how it tastes, how it feels, and why this food satisfies your hunger and gives you pleasure in your head. After going through events, you feel really high and extremely satisfied since you are aware of something that is crucial in every circumstance. In any of these circumstances, we must also be aware that the technique is simple for you. You can easily mingle with the person you loved most, which is why you were surprised when you saw him or her, and you can easily open up with him or her because doing so gives you a mind-free experience. However, in the case of food, scientifically speaking, the food can be digested by your body easily and your body can feel relaxed and energetic after consuming it. Even though there are many well-known foods in the world, you don't buy them; instead, you choose your favourite. We have the spiciest leaves, the richest coffee beans, and the richest Cocoa in the world, but you still choose your favourite since it is easier for your body to digest. Additionally, it is generally simple to get.

As a result, the subject that caught your interest is something you can do easily and you are knowledgeable about. When well-known things are simple to acquire, interest develops. We can observe that a person develops into a superb vocalist because one of his parents is a singer.

> *"Those who cannot work with their hearts achieve but a hollow, half-hearted success that breeds bitterness all around"*
>
> -Dr. A. P. J. Abdul Kalam

Having a businessman as a parent or mother helps a person become a great businessman. The parents of such great people were excellent sources of knowledge. They can very easily find themselves studying those things and unconsciously be drawn to it because they see their parents excelling in that sector and because they are aware of how their parents excel in their careers.

Therefore, when something is easy to obtain, it becomes interesting to you. Do not misunderstand the aforementioned phrase; we too have passions that are entirely distinct from the careers of our parents. However, you still find the key to realising your full potential relatively quickly. Your teacher, your friend's mom, or someone else who inspires you may be the source of this information for you. But compared to how others get the same information, you do it far more easily. And those things are likewise simple for your mind to process. Programming languages are beyond the capabilities of my head, yet aerospace engineering is a big deal. My dad is an offset printer, not an aircraft engineer. However, Dr. A P J Abdul Kalam, one of my inspirations, is someone I admire. My mother inspired me to want to start a business of my own in aerospace technology. Her passion for running her own business is contagious. Despite not being a well-known businessperson, she is a successful one. By learning from my mother's mistakes, I was able to do business with ease. My mother taught me the most important life lesson. Everything was incredibly simple for me to obtain. As a result of my expertise and the ease with which I acquired it, I developed a passion for and interest in the aerospace industry. When you know something and put it into practise, it makes you feel incredibly good.

One additional advice for piqued curiosity, many people questioned me. "Maha! I don't even know one thing that makes me

> *"Don't fear for facing failure in the first attempt. Because even the successful Maths start with Zero"*
>
> *-Dr. A. P. J. Abdul Kalam*

successful; I don't even have a passion for anything. I want to live a prosperous life but I don't know how or where to acquire it, thus I'm living a meaningless existence”. I remarked, "Think my friend, you like something to do in your life. It could be appealing to live like a person you like, whether in terms of appearance, means of support, or line of work. That mind-blowing moment when you first saw the person and your inner voice was saying, "What a guy, I want the same life as him." One of my friends, who comes from a middle-class background and is unable to identify his passion, took out a loan to finish his college education. He is a person who has a degree but no work and a passion for life. However, he revealed to me one day that he wanted to become wealthy in order to lead a successful life because his family was suffering greatly as a result of the student debt, he had taken out to get his degree. You now have a passion, I exclaimed. What are you telling me, he demanded. "Well absolutely buddy, now you got a drive to chase your life to the independence," I replied. Hey friend, start earning money if you want to have complete independence in your life. You're afraid of making money because you lack the drive to pursue your passion and turn it into money. On the other hand, I am aware of your passion. You see, you are one of the millions and millions of people who are currently experiencing the same problem as you. Why can't you, as a teacher, alter yourself to deal with this? Try to turn negatives into benefits. First, try to identify all of your shortcomings and create a real solution for them. Then, after helping those millions of people with your solution, ask for payment for your services.

For example, due of your slothful thinking, you don't have any passion or desire in your life. To become a more active and optimistic person, just battle with your mind and find the solution. — Guess what? He started working as a self-development coach and is now successful. Simple rule: if you lack passion, figure out why. Learn to overcome your weaknesses and establish yourself as an achiever. After a protracted battle with your thoughts, you are given reasons why you should live your life better than you are now doing. "Your life's desire leads you to your passion."

Every person on earth may be absolutely knowledgeable about something or be driven to acquire everything there is to know about it. Any activity is acceptable, including science, math, trade, painting, software, singing, dancing, or even just sitting. Anything almost anything is possible! But it ought to get you so hyped. Your curiosity in the thing is what makes you feel so high. Most people advise following your heart since it knows what you want. Think broadly before following your heart to discover your interests, please! The only thing the heart knows how to pump blood is by producing the lovely lap-tap rhythm of life. Your brain has the ability to think; your heart does not. Your heart is beating as a result of the feelings your brain produces. Find out what makes you so happy and provides you such a high after doing it by following your mind and brain (your brain's operating system). My friend, it is your area of interest, and everyone will notice you since you are so much higher than everybody else. Because you are at the top of your game, it will set you out from others. When you perform at your best. So, find your Interest!

Find your interest!

You can quickly identify your interests by providing answers to the questions below.

Where do you spend most of your money? - The majority of the money spent by those who are seriously interested in sports goes toward the purchase of sporting goods and accessories. People who enjoy music will typically purchase items that are related to music.

What do you do when you're free? - What kinds of posts catch your attention on social media if you're just skimming through it? We typically choose to go on outings, gather, and watch movies in our free time. We only prefer to go through social media throughout the workweek to chill. We only pick the things that interests us, when we are bored with all of these above activities or when we want to fill our free time with something particularly intriguing. When you are simply going through social media, a certain item catches your attention for a while because you are genuinely interested in it.

What activity do you spend a lot of time on without even realising it? – When we are engaged in activities that truly interest us, we become aware that time is passing quickly. For instance, you may feel that the time you are spending with your loved ones is insufficient. If you enjoy travelling, the days will not be enough for you. since you can do so without getting agitated.

Which of your past accomplishments made you feel particularly proud? – When you do a task in which you have a genuine interest, you will be overjoyed and proud of yourself. For instance, if you are a YouTuber, you won't become bored when making the content. You feel so proud of yourself after sharing it. You meticulously crafted the content because you loved doing it. You gradually increase your work quality as a result.

List an action you took in the past that gained applauses. – You will become more well-known after completing the task that interests you. Their admiration for your work will grow. because you are moulding your creation. You put a lot of love and interest into everything you do.

1.2. Find Knowledge

"Interest – Practise – Continuous Action – Knowledge/Skill – Money"

The Moment I Realized the power of place…

When I was trying to establish my credibility, I heard a brief narrative that helped me see things differently. Camel and its calf are the subject of the tale. The mother camel and her youngster are seated beneath the tree one day. Why do we have lengthy legs, the calf questioned his mother. We dwell in a desert that is full of sand, the mother camel said. We have long legs that allow us to move easily in a sand pit. Calf once more questioned his mother, "Why do we have a hump?" Mother said, "We live in a desert where it is difficult to find water." We therefore have hump in our body to store the water for subsequent usage. The last and most crucial question was then posed by the calf to the mother camel: why are we here at the zoo then? —— Camel has the ability to endure in desert areas. Even though camels are useless since they have the extraordinary ability to thrive in the desert rather than living in a zoo. See how this short story has a powerful lesson. My entire life has been altered by this story. I am aware of something incredibly special, but I am unsure of how to make it public so that it can be recognised.

"With great knowledge at wrong place will not be a good thing".

The moment I realized what is knowledge…

Another event in my life helped me to clearly realise what knowledge is. I once went to see an offset printing business. A single elderly man was working nearby a large group of young men. Although those young men were working nonstop, I could see that they had several distractions. A very small number of people are working completely and devotedly, while others are distracted by their phones, talking to nearby co-workers, or waiting for their break. That elderly man is one of those hardworking employees. I tell you what. His work and his pace of work astounded me. He was where the papers were being pasted. His task is to take a card, glue it, and then place another piece of paper on top of it to create a single piece of card. Thus, there are roughly three steps to the work: take a card and place it, add glue, and then add paper. He was continuously working on this. Due to his consistent hard work, the elderly guy became an expert at precisely pasting a card. Nobody there could perform as well as that elderly man. You know what, he was a gifted and knowledgeable worker who put a lot of effort into his profession. Nevertheless, he received a far lower wage than other employees. This brutality only befell the elderly guy because of his advanced age and the fact that he was using his ability on someone who had no idea how valuable it was. When I questioned him about his employment history, he replied that he had been employed for the previous 53 years. He had extensive knowledge in offset printing, from the initial paper loading until the last paste. He was able to do all tasks for other processes including designing, ordering spare parts, and accounting because he had been working with his boss for about 53 years. On behalf of his boss, he adhered to everything. In the same way that most bosses do, his boss took advantage of his goodness and diligence. You are probably now thinking, "If he had the initiative to start his own business, he may currently be a successful businessman in printing technology." I claim you are mistaken. Do you know the reason? I have encountered that elderly man, but you may encounter another elderly person. Some individuals may encounter another elderly person in popular social media posts. Therefore, there are a lot of diligent people in the globe. There are several printing businesses situated in the same stretch of that neighbourhood, but I observed an old offset printing company and chose to use their services. Each company has a representative who is similar to the elderly man who has worked there for ten years. I might see someone else in that situation if the elderly man is not present. You can say, "Maha, isn't he working really hard. He has talent for his work as well. Why are you claiming that if he begins his own business, he would fail? See, my buddy, we bathe and wash our teeth every day. Tell me, is it a skill you have or a habit? When you

> *"Without involvement you can't succeed. With your involvement you can't fail"*
>
> *-Dr. A. P. J. Abdul Kalam*

practice a task repeatedly, it becomes incredibly effortless for you, but depending on the outcome, it will either be seen as a talent or a habit. Whether an action develops into a habit or a skill relies on how it impacts your way of life. For instance: When a musician practises music every day, it comes naturally to him or her. Due to its skill, it is having a significant impact on his profession and giving him a successful business. Another illustration: A carpenter using the same tools to cut, shape, and fix wood produces beautiful crafts or designs for wooden objects. He practises the same thing every day, and it becomes second nature to him as it develops into skill. Another example is a worker who fixes bolt and nut assemblies every day in the extremely large vehicle manufacturing industry. He does it in a repetitious manner until it becomes habit. For your clear comprehension, I used the terms classic profession and typical career. You should know that the careers of music and carpentry are at the extreme ends of the job spectrum. Increasing skill at the same thing every day provides significant knowledge. Consider the worker; he is merely performing the same tasks as the elderly man who I once knew who was pasting paper cards while fixing bolts and nuts. They are improving their effectivity, efficiency, productivity, and quality of work via the actions they are taking. Despite the fact that they are making money from these behaviours, they are not having a significant impact on their lives. Being completely honest, workers in the car sector and elderly man produce high-quality work when they perform habitable tasks for comparable long-term lower pay. However, when a musician or a carpenter does the same thing every day, it increases both the quality of their work and their level of creativity, giving it a distinctive quality and resulting in significant financial gain. You are aware that as we increase our knowledge or skills, our income should increase. Some people will say, "I am doing these things for my happiness not for money". Damn no one will be like that, because it is clear that making money is the primary motivation behind everything we have examined so far in this book. The only reason to develop an interest, begin studying, begin practising, and ultimately start a business is money. Of course, we should be happy with our careers, and I wholeheartedly agree. But money is still important. The key, though, is money, and in order to get it, we must be able to differentiate habit and knowledge according to its impact in life and in order to get it, we must be able to tell one habit from another, and our knowledge must take into account the influence of each. We may improve our quality of life by using our talent and expertise to earn more money, in my opinion. If you still don't agree with what I've said, then tell me: are you working on a project or providing a service that fully satisfies you? If you said "yes," I also need you to confirm "would you do that job/service for someone for free in the long run?"

Haha. Your response is one I already know. "NO" is your response. Since you are reading this book by yourself, don't be afraid to be completely honest with yourself. Only us both are in communication. With me, you can have an open mind.

The moment I realized scarcity of knowledge…

I was having a talk with my friend's father one day. While he was observing me, my friend's family was talking to his father about me, my passion, my level of knowledge, and everything else. Father has a tendency to be arrogant. Though he believes he already knows everything, he is a terrific speaker. I felt quite confident in my technical expertise, as well as my leadership and interpersonal skills, because I am incredibly enthusiastic about aeronautical engineering and entrepreneurship. He started talking to me and telling me about himself and his past. How he will conduct himself in every aspect of his profession. I'm a good listener as well as a guarded speaker. I was hearing what he was saying. While we were talking, he inquired about ISRO, the government-run space research agency of India. He challenged me with the question, "Where is the ISRO launch pad located?" Sri Hari Kotta, I said. He questioned me once more, this time asking where Sri Hari Kotta is. Sometimes we are aware of the solutions but struggle to recall them fast. It took our brain a few seconds to retrieve the unnecessary information that had been stored therein. I was therefore unable to respond. I am aware that it is in the state of Andhra. He laughed at me, which seemed shameful to me. You are a child who calls yourself an intelligent, He disrespectfully told me to do a lot of research because I didn't know anything and needed to do so much of it. Well, just like me, everyone may encounter situations of this nature in the classroom, during a family event, a gathering of friends, a department meeting, etc. Someone who is similar to the father of my friend might ask you a question that is not at all important at the time. He embarrassed you in front of the crowds. When you were learning stock marketing, for instance, he might have asked you, "How many enterprises are there in stock markets?" I know it's ridiculous, right? He will insult you in front of the crowd despite the fact that you are unaware of the solution. However, you are aware of your intelligence and your aptitude for the material you are learning for your professional advancement. However, while you are currently being insulted, you might be thinking that you lack the skills necessary for trading business. After this point, the majority of people stop learning. Few people will respond to him in such a way that demonstrates their worth and ability to handle such a task. However, my friend, if you are typical of most people, then this is for you. Instead of learning how to turn on the burner, we need to practise and learn how much salt to add to a dish. I'll be honest and say that at first, I felt as most people do, but later I learned that I needed to practise and learn how to season my dish, (which is termed "AERO-INTEL" and refers to my knowledge of aerospace engineering). It will be acceptable in my situation if he asks me how to turn on the stove. But he questioned, "Do you know what a stove is?" Thank God for opening my eyes, Haha!

The moment I realized what is my knowledge…

Although I have a degree in nanotechnology, I founded my own business and rose to the position of chief aerospace engineer. I was working as a trainer for a month at a 3D modelling training facility one day. On that day, they held a competition where students had to present papers. I was seated as an observer. One lovely girl was discussing aerospace, particularly space travel. But she missed something crucial in terms of communication strategy. In that instant, I became so haughty that I confronted her because I understood more than she did. I didn't hesitate to confront her in front of the room's more than fifty guests, and I expressed the concept to everyone there.

Here is small advice, "Being arrogant takes everything from us. Being kind brings anything to us."

Another example: I'm a talented artist who enjoys black and white pencil drawings. I'm not sure the name I'm using to describe this style of drawing is appropriate, but I think you get the idea. We are four individuals conversing about sketching while seated in a room. I said absolutely nothing about drawing. I am able to produce flawless and exquisite pencil drawings, but I am unable to bring about the communication between art and the human through the drawing.

You know what, I have a keen interest in both pencil drawing and aerospace engineering. Without a time, limit, I can complete both tasks. You know what, even though I'm good at both and really interested in both, I agree that my only area of expertise is in aerospace engineering and not drawing. We need to have a thorough understanding of my two life events. Due to my expertise in the subject, I was able to speak confidently in front of a crowd of strangers in the first instance. I can explain anything to everyone in detail. However, in the second event, despite the fact that I am a talented artist, I was unable to express a single word in front of only four people because I was unsure of how to approach the painting. I'm quite confused about drawing techniques, and I'm not sure I can compete with the top artists in the world. I have a variety of interests that are distinct from one another, and I can give each of them my all. However, I can only be an expert in one. One remark that one of my professors said stands out in my memory. He constantly told me that, while we may study anything, we should focus on becoming experts in only one field. Like one of Bruce Lee's well-known quotes, *"I fear not the man who practised 10,000 kicks once, But I fear the man who has practised one kick 10,000 times"*.

We can therefore pursue a variety of interests, such as speaking, sketching, working, etc. However, we fall short in every area of our interest. And don't worry, we don't need to excel in a variety of areas. As an illustration, I can envision many South Indian actors doing the principal roles while also singing, dancing, and writing lyrics. However, while receiving significant remuneration and accolades, they are not treated as masters. Pay and awards are getting on the basis of reach among audiences. The all-rounder product will have a wide audience reach, but it may be interchangeable, people will forget their work while days go. However, a master's output will become unerasable in history if they exclusively concentrate on one skill. We have great legends who are concentrating on just one skill; they cannot be replaced by all-arounders. This is the power of concentrating on just one skill as opposed to concentrating on several things at once.

Discover your area of interest where you excel. The subject matter you are extremely passionate about and well-versed in is the one on which you are very strong, enjoy speaking in front of audiences, enjoy correcting others' errors in it, create alternative solutions or creative ways to carry out operations. So, find your knowledge!

Find your knowledge!

List out the interest of you. – We may have several interests. Make a list of all the activities or jobs that make you happy.

Pick one topic from your interest and prepare for the presentation lecture, to teach about the innovative approach to replace the traditional one.

1.3. Be Paid

Take your time and think back to all I have covered in earlier topics. You discovered your area of expertise and treasured the knowledge that related to it. You might be asking, is this book pointing in the correct direction at this point. Do I really need to monetize my passion? Is it acceptable if I use my passion for financial gain? Because a lot of yogis, spiritual authorities, self-help books, public figures, morality tales, motion pictures, leaders, your family, and friends all advise you to pursue happiness. Never follow the money. You already know the secret; people are getting pay for doing things like posting articles or videos on social media, speaking in front of an audience, running webinars, or serving public speaking on the above regards. Spiritual authorities and yogis of days appear affluent. But not me or you, who are listening, observing, and soaking in all the morals, laws, and guidelines they are giving us. I'm not religious, but you should know that I'm a highly spiritual person. Even I believe that the adage "Money makes anything" is true. because of the really difficult financial times my family and I suffered. Awfully terrible. Every successful person will claim, "I went through the fire like life, made me zero." However, my family and I were destroyed by the volcano, turning into negative values rather than zero. but only in terms of finances, not mental fortitude. Thanks to my mother and father, who raised me with a lot of kindness and respect, I was able to keep my silence during some of the most difficult periods and when I was being disrespected in public. You simply cannot imagine that circumstance.

> *"This is my belief: that through difficulties and problems God gives us the opportunity to grow. So, when your hopes and dreams and goals are dashed, search among the wreckage, you may find a golden opportunity hidden in the ruins"*
>
> *-Dr. A. P. J. Abdul Kalam*

That circumstance is the primary factor that motivated me to take the actions I do now, made me think, and raised me. The driving force behind all events is money. Therefore, I advise, you can chase money by chasing your happiness. Understand clearly, I'm not saying that, chase your happiness by chase money. If I express it that way, it conveys the message that having money is essential for happiness. It renders the entirety of what I described in this book incorrect. Chase happiness while pursuing money, rather chase happiness by pursuing money, in my opinion. You may be satisfied with what you are doing with your life and make money at the same time, after all. Because of this, I'm telling you that it's okay to chase money. When you have enough money for yourself and your family, you can pursue happiness, a spiritual life, serenity, and an unending life, sadhu/yogi life. But keep in mind that even those intelligent individuals – Sadhus/yogis are getting pay in lakhs as a fee, by claiming that to maintain your consistency in their class.

"Money is a key to grow"

Consider, my friend, that you are reading this book in order to make money. And I'm going to demonstrate to you how to follow your passion and make money in a real, ethical way. But keep in mind that no matter who purchases your goods or services, we should always bring values to them. Great value, high profits. Therefore, it is acceptable to pursue your desire for money if it brings you happy. So, be paid!

1.4. Match Knowledge - Demand

In various sources, including social media, we have n-number of information, contents to increase our knowledge as well as become worthless people. But each piece of content either worth or worthless has a distinct audience and generates a separate business. In order to improve my product creations, I also spend some time looking through social media. But I continue to make an effort to spend less time on social media. I want to investigate my level of creativity, my capacity for thought, and my level of productivity. We have a wealth of educational materials on the internet and in print, but we also have derogatory, harmful, and pointless material. For instance, in one YouTube video I recently watched, a boy is just sitting still for whole video. It's a kind of very long video completely useless video that gives viewers no information, right? I'm not saying it's a bad one; rather, I'm saying it's useless. However, it is also creating a side business, using your data (which is a business), increasing the number of hours people watch the video (which is also a business), and most intriguingly, some other entertaining social media channels are using this video as the basis for their own troll content, which is a side business that is making money. Funny, but do you know something? I subsequently discovered that many yoga instructors and spiritual gurus receive thousands and even millions of dollars from individuals just to instruct others on how to remain still and maintain mental peace. Now, I can hear you saying, "WHAT!!!!" in your head. Haha…... Therefore, always bear in mind that everything you learn and everything you teach is beneficial. The important thing is that it should add value to people's lives.

You can see advertisements from a variety of persons promising to teach you how to become a millionaire, a bestselling author, or a rich online educator. You know what, I went to one of the services mentioned above. This webinar is for a fee. The webinar is actually pretty nice, but the host hinted that the most important thing to remember is to "try to do like me," invite people to study "how to become a billionaire" like what he is doing, and train them to make a course on the subject. But he also offers a few mentorships, contacts to investors, and marketing techniques for highlighting the extra values for people and distinctive selling points of their services. However, many individuals aren't going to understand the fundamental concept he implied to his audiences hiddenly. Very few people will successfully decipher the secret code and become millionaires. However, the webinar host makes millions of dollars. Naturally, there are many audiences available to learn proper entrepreneurship! Oh wrong, I should not have said that the popularity of entrepreneurship development courses gave you the impression that you could get paid. But in that case, I'm fine. I must do my part to help you succeed. I'm happy to see you an entrepreneurship mentor.

Again, wait Oh, that sounds like your inner voice saying, "Maha! You advised me to build values for individuals in order to increase my pay, but I'm still a little confused. In addition, you claim that sub-businesses and useless material are both very profitable. How can I decide clearly? Well, my friend, I have the solution. I'll demonstrate to you how to earn money in a real and efficient method by giving enormous value to people, as I promised. You understand that each type of information has a different audience, right? All we have to do is match demand with our knowledge. I've noticed that a lot of people make the mistake of believing that this type of business has a very large niche while in fact it just has a small one. My friend, the population of the planet is enormous. Everyone is ingesting food, drinking beverages, roaming about, travelling, and sleeping. For every decision we make and action we do, there is need of technology or products. For instance, the globe is your market if you want to manufacture inventive toothbrushes. The general online population is your specialty if you want to produce entertaining video material for online platforms. However, the fact remains that individuals demand variations in each good or service, period. Take tooth brush cases as an example. Some require a toothbrush and a tongue cleaner, others demand soft bristles, others the smallest, the cheapest, or the most colourful. Not everyone has the same objectives. If everyone has the same needs, there will only be a few brands for all goods and services. All goods and services must meet the diverse demands of people. Better quality and improvements are required by people. We have many brands for the same product and service because of this. Therefore, I'm suggesting that every piece of information you produce and every piece of knowledge you learn in order to grow a product/service has a certain specialty and target market. Bring your business to your niche—that is the crucial thing to remember here. We also need to be aware that a new age group is being formed every day. Every day, a new person turns 23, and every day, someone gets tired of using their current one and wants to buy a new one to replace the damaged one. I'll emphasize that the important thing is to target your market with your business.

Choosing your business is the only action you need to do. You have question again right, "How do I choose my business," is correct. The answer is that you are aware of some of your hobbies and that there is just one area in which you are highly knowledgeable. For example, you enjoy trading and can instruct people in trading because you are an expert in it. You therefore want to produce content related to your interests, such as an online course. You can currently easily make money from anywhere by taking an online course, which is one of the booming businesses of the 2020s. I offered you a few illustrations of people demanding from various fields, including engineering, trade, and design. There are distinct audiences for each one. As you can see from the picture below,

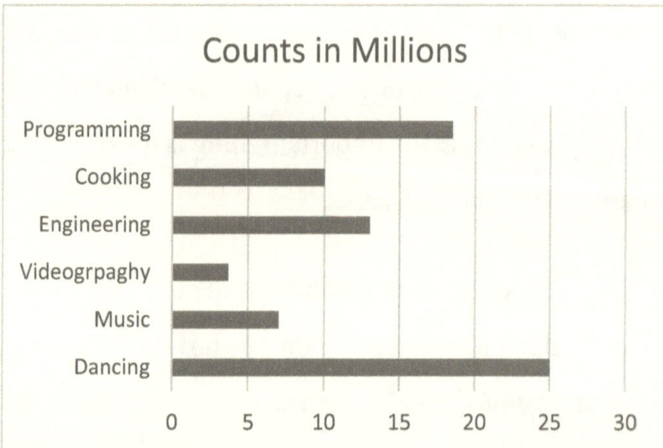

As the picture displays the facts through 2022, I hope you now have a better understanding of how much demand there is in each industry. Every field has its own set of audiences, just as in the

aforementioned examples. When your course has excellent contents and if it covers nearly all the aspects, those who are as passionate about the subject as you are would undoubtedly buy it. You only need to devote a single shift of your time to earn money for the rest of your life. The number of enrolments will rise day by day, generating your passive revenue. However, one thing you should do is include the right keywords and course categories while creating the online course to meet demand and attract more customers. You realise how simple it is? I can see that even teenagers are earning money by selling their online courses. In 2020, I visited a college in India, where I observed a professor in a senior position within that department. He uses a single, extremely basic laptop to complete his work. You know, he is actually 45 years old, works as a college professor, but he still finds it difficult to support himself financially at the moment. He holds a doctorate by then. In 1997, he received his university degree. According to my estimation, he must have spent over

50,000 INR on his education, nearly 14,600 INR for housing during the graduation period, and he must have spent 5,000 INR travelling to various institutions and businesses to get additional expertise. Finally, he may have to spend 10,000 INR on additional paperwork, notebooks, and library fees. So, he paid about 79,600 INR for his four years of university. He then continued to pursue his Masters and Ph.D. degrees while spending close to 4,00,000 INR to become a doctor. He currently makes 33,000 INR each month. As I write this book in 2022, roadside small store proprietors can easily make 40,000 INR without a large investment. They only need 1000-10,000 INR to get started. What is the need to invest 4,00,000 INR to become a teacher in order to earn 33,000 INR? Nonetheless, students between the ages of 18 and 20 are studying from that professor and developing their own online course, which allows them to make more than he does; however, this is just another source of passive income for those students. They are not even a grown person; they are only a teenager in the learning stage who has begun earning. So, I see the professor's difficulty as being that he is delivering his business to a little market. He is only covering about 40 students inside the classroom. If he covers a wide audience, he can easily earn lakhs as a passive income. Another life experience, I mentioned that roadside vendors can easily make 40,000 INR. I also stated that they simply needed to invest 1000-10,000 INR in their firm. Most of you will disagree with me. Because our civilization raised us in this manner. We cannot run a firm without funding. It is, in my opinion, entirely incorrect. Because we can start a business with "ZERO" investment or with very little investment, very little very little.

"Best Business starts with ZERO"

I can hear your mind saying, "How are you so sure about this Maha!" Well, I am that roadside vendor; I invested only 1000 INR and made 40,000 INR in one month. You're intrigued, aren't you? Haha.... I know you can generate money without any investment, without a university degree, and without any prior expertise. Yes, most people used to say that we couldn't achieve anything without experience. But I believe you can. Let me explain in detail how I made 40,000 INR with only a 1000 INR investment. My mother is an excellent cook. Her chicken biryani dish is excellent. Nobody in my town makes a finer chicken biryani, as far as I can tell. I had no prior experience in the hotel business, but I had planned to open a biryani eatery in my town. I grabbed one table and chair from my house and placed it in a very populated neighbourhood. I spent 1000 INR on ingredients for chicken biryani. My mother would prepare chicken biryani in the utensils she currently has at home. I make the decision to sell for 100Rs. Nobody in my town is selling for this low a price. They are retailing for 150Rs and will have a very limited number, as well as a bad flavour. I gave 100Rs worth of chicken biryani. We can serve 10 people with 1 kilogramme of biryani. So, by selling ten Chicken Biryanis, we may earn 1000INR. We can produce 2 kilos of Chicken Biryani for 1000 INR. So, at the end of the day, I can make a profit of 2000 INR. My investment was 1000Rs. I earned 2000INR in returns, thus my profit for the day is 1000 Rs. I don't have to pay rent to shopkeepers. At the end of the month, I made 40,000 INR by progressively increasing the quantity of chicken biryani, although every day I used to give out 2-3 biryani for free to hungry needy people. See, I didn't pay for the space, nor did I pay for the cooking equipment; I simply purchased raw meat, vegetables, and rice to cook with. That's it. In India, 40,000INR is enough to live a comfortable lower-middle-class life. But I need to start a big business so that I can provide for myself and my family financially. I spent two months without a shop and earned a lakh before investing in a premium biryani shop in a high-tech city where I can earn more easily. My family is now taking care of my Chicken Biryani business. And I'm concentrating on my aerospace industry. What I've done is simply match the knowledge with the demand, and despite the fact that it's a traditional business, it's paying me well.

The best-selling business is created by combining all three important factors. Interest, understanding, and demand Not everyone possesses in-demand skills such as programming, engineering,

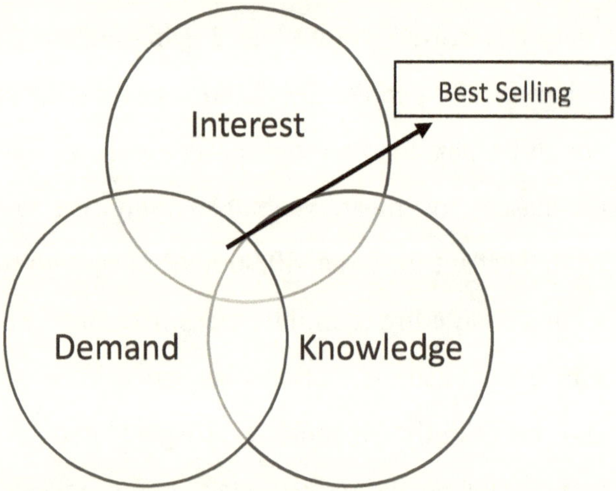

app development, web development, trading, and marketing, but each skill has its own demand. Consider yourself: you learned about your field of interest and gained knowledge, right? Why did you want to learn about that particular one? Of course, you are interested in it, but the reality is that, that one thing has created some values in your life or career. So, the knowledge added value to you, and you created a demand for it by learning it. This is a big world, and you have a lot of opportunities for creating your own audience for your knowledge area. Because there are many people who share your interest. As I previously stated, not everyone is looking for the same thing. But, as I previously stated, everyone is looking for the same thing. Don't get the two statements mixed up; some people will have the same interest, but they will require different quality, level/quantity, size, price, and so on. Using the same example of a toothbrush, some people looked for soft bristles, while others looked for a brush with a tongue cleaner. However, both groups of people are looking for the common toothbrush. So, if both sets of your niche are looking for the same product, you need to bring advancement or increase the value you provide them because they are looking for different sub-categories. If you want to attract both groups of people, you must create a third category that is more efficient than the first two. I know you know what is in your best interests at this point, and you are one step closer to making money from your knowledge. You only need to do one thing: Match knowledge and demand!

PHASE 2

LEARNING

2
PAHSE LEARNING

"Learning gives creativity,
Creativity leads to thinking,
Thinking leads to knowledge,
Knowledge makes you great."

- Dr. A. P. J. Abdul Kalam

At this point, you know what your interests are and which ones you know a lot about. You are now in PHASE 2 of the process. You will learn about learnings during this phase. In this PHASE 2, you will investigate the learning process and how to master it. But you know what? I'm going to show you how to make money from our passion while we're still learning. I can hear your mind say. "Maha! is this some sort of joke?" So, my friend, I'm serious; I'll show you how to make money from our business while we're still learning. So, hello and welcome to PHASE 2!

2.1. I'm Learning, but what?

Starting the learning process is a beautiful part of the journey. We can explore ourselves, bring new ideas, and give different ways of thinking when we begin our learning process. You may obtain many people's contacts and support in order to expand your knowledge, which will have an impact on your future career. When I was still learning, I just started one of my businesses, which is an online education business. You may be wondering how I started the online education business while still in the learning stage. I'll explain later in this book.

I went to one aerospace industry during my learning stage because I am passionate about aerospace engineering. There, I discovered a multitude of educational opportunities in the aerospace industry. I had an interesting conversation with the CEO of that company. Following our final conversation, He was given me the opportunity to merge my online education business with his. I was mystified because we couldn't get this kind of opportunity at the start of our business. It is a significant one for aspiring business owners. This opportunity compelled me to learn, and I learned so much about my passion; it gave me the opportunity to learn what I wanted to learn and what people needs to learn. Life provided me with an easy way to comprehend the demand for my passion. I achieved mastery. Every business focuses on a specific niche, but that niche also has its own sub-categories. As seen in the tooth brush business example. But we must first understand what this world truly requires. What value should we add to the world to make it a better place? For example, in the 1990s, people preferred to watch mild dramas and dramatic films. However, we are now entering the realm of virtual reality. People's expectations of cinema experiences are increasing year after year, creating new demand. So, learning is not a bad thing; anything we learn will undoubtedly help us in the future. However, not everyone wishes to learn everything. For example, IT professionals who use the same programming language for web development, app development, and UI/UX design. However, they are learning the common programming language. They want to learn web development, app development, and other related skills. When it comes to drawing, some people excel at portraiture, while others excel at comics, pencil sketches, water painting, and abstract painting. In the food industry, some people prefer Chinese cuisine, others prefer Indian cuisine, still others prefer Thailand, and so on. So learning is not bad, but we must ensure that our learning is actually demanded. We have a syllabus in our university degree that follows a traditional procedure, but industries are actually working to advance, so they only need people who are up to date. As a result, students demanded that they learn current technologies and techniques/methods outside of universities. So, in order to grow our business significantly, we must learn in-demand skills. So, understand that demand is nothing more than a customer's requirement. In other words, demand is the current trend. Progress is inevitable. Advancements create a new trend, and the new trend produces demand.

"Time let us to do business on what we know"

My friend! We should be very clear about what we are going to learn. Because learning requires a significant investment of time, energy, and money. Learning is our backbone. Learning will make us successful; learning will provide us with a way to make money, and learning will make us indelible in history. As a matter of fact, we must be very specific about what we are learning. The beauty of learning is that it never stops for the rest of our lives.

"Learning never stops"

All the way from the stone age to the age of the Internet, we have made progress through continuous learning. During my graduation period, I attended a lecture. My professor asked me to describe the current trends in my field. I explained him in front of my entire class. It was typical that after my speech, they moved on to the next topic. But that one moment changed my entire learning mindset. During my graduation, I thought professors were legends in their fields, knowing everything there is to know. Even they can come up with the best innovations until that one moment arrives. A few days after my speech, the professor who had asked me to share current trends called up me to his cabin. He and I talked about one of the topics I mentioned in my speech. You know what, I'm not sure about that technology, but I still gave everyone a speech. But my professor is very interested in what I knew at the time, and he said, "After your speech, I went to search about that technology, and it is actually not a possible technology, it is completely a fiction one." Please conduct additional research if you have the time. Make it very clear what you are learning. Especially when instructing others. I was guilty. I asked him, sir, why you did research on my speech. He stated, "I found that it is not possible tech while you speak that." So, I decided to clarify myself first, so that I could correct you. I wanted to conduct research on your speech to get a clear picture. That one is now crystal clear to you. I know you're a good teacher with a lot of knowledge, but you should be very clear when you're learning and teaching. I guessed that if I devote some time to you, it will be extremely beneficial to your career. That is why, my boy. Actually, I was taken aback. He shaped my entire professional life. At that point, I realised that I needed to be very clear while learn and teach what people wanted to learn, because my teaching would have a huge impact on their lives. As a result, our learning and teaching should add value to the lives of others. And providing value is the main key for successful people. If you want to add value to the world with your product or service, you must stay current. Now you must determine what the trend is. In various fields, a trend is not an ongoing fashion. A trend is actually a current human need. For example, in the nineties, people wanted to send mail letters to communicate with their loved ones. So, they needed a postman to deliver their letters, and the process of delivering the post required perfect management. When the post office was established, it served the people by delivering their mail. As ordinary citizens, we only need to be aware that our letters are being delivered by the post office. However, as a businessperson, you should have detailed knowledge of each process and the value it generates. The post office provides people with job opportunities and values their employees. Because it is a government job, they receive a pension after they retire. The office requires a management asset, while the postman requires a cycle to obtain deals from outside traders. Postmen can now deliver anywhere in the world. However, a new issue has arisen. Letters are not delivered on time; private post sectors were created, and they added much more value to the people by delivering the post as quickly as possible. We now use e-mails and social applications to connect everyone in a split second, as if the entire world were in our hands. Year after year, the demand for only one factor, fast communication, grows. Every year, there is progress. People's expectations are also increasing, creating a demand. We cannot satisfy the people if we continue to learn the traditional technique. We should be ahead of the curve, and our vision should be far beyond the present.

I enjoy learning and am still learning and expanding my knowledge of my passion to become a godfather in it. I will undoubtedly serve as a godfather. But consistency is essential, and we must accept that we do not know everything and that we can learn from anyone, even a child. This mental state is the foundation for attaining the god state of learning (Speaking spiritually). So, I'm learning and you?

2.2. Art of Master:

Being a master is an art. We should sculpt ourselves step by step in order to become an "Art of Master." By following the steps, I discussed in this phase, I was able to become a master in aerospace engineering in just 6 months. I am very interested in aerospace engineering, so I decided to learn everything I could about the industry. I eventually started applying for jobs in various aerospace industries was given one interview opportunity. I have already completed various internships in various aerospace industries, but they are insufficient for me because they do not meet the demand and do not provide me with valuable insights. You might be thinking right now, "Maha! Why did you choose to learn from industries? You have plenty of opportunities to learn outside!" Yes, you are correct! I made a mistake. I reasoned that if I joined the aerospace industry, I would be able to easily understand what they were doing and what real problems industries were facing at the time, allowing me to direct my career in that direction. Through my startup, I can create the new development. When I visited that company, I noticed that they attempted to solve every engineering problem mathematically. Of course, everyone enjoys it. But the problem is that I am not a mathematician. So, I decided to learn the mathematical approach to aerospace engineering. I pursued numerous industries and internships, but no one provided me with that knowledge. And I came to the conclusion that all engineering students want to learn mathematical approaches. So, having discovered a demand, I need to develop a solution as a product or service to provide great value to my students. It was the initial motivation for me to start an online educational business. I researched various platforms, discovered various books with various approaches, and simplified it for myself. Aerospace is a vast field; we cannot learn in this manner. As a result, I decided to divide it into several smaller parts. I jotted down what I knew, what I didn't know, and everything else in my notebook. This article gave me a clear understanding of what I know and what I need to know to become a master. Thank God, I chose the aerospace industry, where I already had some experience, because it made my learning process so much easier. If you choose what is best for you, you can simplify and ease your learning process.

My father always told me to keep written notes for whatever I was learning. Make a note of it whenever a new idea strikes you. I have personal notes, handwritten formats of my knowledge, and sticky notes on my working and learning areas for anything I don't know and need to learn and things which are to be completed at first in a list. These sticky notes are a constant reminder to me to learn. As a matter of fact, "Words Are My Motivators." You know what, having a clear idea about the topic you want to learn provides you with a focused path to learning. If you divide the path into milestones, you will find it easier to learn. Step-by-step improvement sculpts you into a perfect "Art of Master." These milestones are nothing more than your syllabus for learning about your interest. The art of learning is in structuring the syllabus. You may be aware that the majority of successful syllabus creators are paid for the structure of the syllabus. Everything, you see, is a business. We can make money just by structuring the syllabus. I enjoy planning the syllabus. I developed a structured curriculum for learning aerospace engineering, and you know what? I'm using the same curriculum for my online educational business too. Because that is the value I created in my life, and I wanted to provide the same or even better value to my students; it gives me the same satisfaction as caring for children. I always treat my trainees and students as if they were my children, even if they are older than me. *One of my gurus taught me to be the parent of all creation in the universe. Being a parent to all creations entails a great deal of responsibility.* To create a syllabus, we must first understand the entire scope of the subject. I wrote down all of the basic terms, concepts, important principles, pros and cons, and applications that I am already familiar with. Then I wrote down what I needed to know, such as current trends, advancements, and future scope. Finally, after rearranging everything, I had a perfect syllabus. Please see the image below to get a better idea of my syllabus structure. I divided the topics into three levels: beginner, intermediate, and professional. We have these three levels in any field.

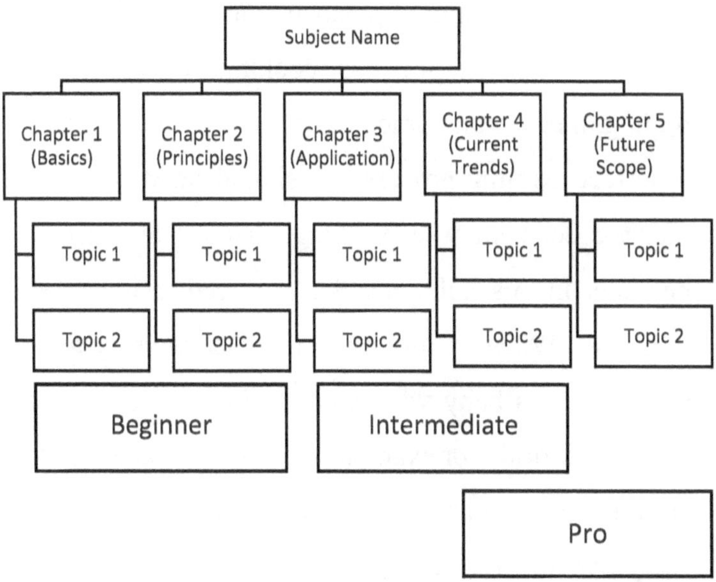

See, before we begin the learning process, we must first clearly understand one thing. As I previously stated, we have extensive knowledge in one area of particular interest in which we are eager to learn. The truth is that before beginning the structured learning process, we were still at the very beginning. Of course, we know advanced techniques and current trends, and we can teach others. But, in reality, when asked to do the thing practically, we couldn't. Even if you share the same interest in what your family is doing, in practise, you can't. You can take any subject, such as cooking, drawing, or trading, and without practise, we are nothing. To get a perfect learning process, we should be very clear that we don't know everything, that we are just a beginner in this field, and that we need to improve ourselves. When we are in this mindset, we may feel as if we are a baby who wants to know everything about the world. For example, we can see that a small baby always asks us about everything she sees. But as she grows older, she stops asking us why things are happening the way they are. This is because she began learning from herself, and another reason is that she felt burdened when she began learning the things. I actually remember my science teacher allowing us to see a microscopic image of our human cells when I was in fourth grade. It appears to be a pinkish hexagonal structure. I was curious about bio-science after that live experience. But as I got older in school, I began to dislike biology because I couldn't find myself interested in it. I think it's just because the other science teacher taught me in a way that made it difficult for me to understand. You can ask me how you know your teacher does not have adequate teaching skills. You may recall that my fourth-grade science teacher gave me the opportunity to observe the human cell in action. That was the first time I had ever seen a human cell, and it will be the last. I've never seen any cells, bacteria, or fungi at a microscopic level, which is required in middle school. That is why I say my teachers has a poor teaching ability. For example, if I say something about an unknown object that you haven't heard, you can't picture what I'm talking about. Our brain begins to think about the visual of the new object by recalling previously stored data. Then how can you imagine a new object that you have never seen before? If we were a baby in this situation, we would undoubtedly hate the subject. As I mentioned in phase 1, what we can easily obtain will help spark our interest. So, if we are like a baby who begins learning when everything is easy to access by our brain, we can easily make ourselves good learners through this learning journey by breaking everything down into easy smaller parts. I'm confident in this because I am the living example. This is the path I took to become a Master of Aerospace Engineering. You know what, I am the average, and sometimes the last, student in my school. However, because I used this syllabus method to learn during my diploma and degree, I became one of the toppers in my department. These small small inputs gave me time to think and gave my brain plenty of time to recollect, rethink, and find innovative/creative alternatives.

I provided a straightforward approach to syllabus arrangement in the preceding syllabus structure. Let me share one of my syllabising courses experiences. I created a live Nanotechnology course in which I included basic quantum mechanics laws and principles, nanomaterial preparation methods and FEA, and nanomaterial applications. That is, I covered all of the sub-divisions in a single live course. After completing a course, I received feedback from the students, with some who didn't know about nanotech saying they learned something new and advanced, while those who did said it was a good course but very basic. So, to give you a clear picture of my experience, even though I covered everything from basic to application level, 1% of people thought it was basic. Even if it is a small number, we must solve the problem in order to have a profitable and reliable business. It is not necessary to solve the problem here. The question is why these differences were felt by those 1% of the people. When you are a beginner, you may feel excited or interested because you are in the early stages of learning. If you are an intermediate or a pro, repeating the same thing like basic will bore you. Thus, creating a syllabus is critical in order to have a consistent learning journey. At the beginner level, you should cover all of the fundamental terms and concepts, with some application examples. If my middle school teacher had given me the opportunity to learn practically, I might have become a doctor or biologist. Oh, my goodness, she didn't. Now I'm writing this book for you. Well, conceptual and application-based research entices people to learn more and provides a clear understanding. Intermediate level students should have a thorough understanding of their subject. It also includes the progression section. Don't cover basic concepts and ideas at the pro level; instead, dive right into the big problem-solving techniques and advancements. It should be entirely based on practical learnings; people should do things practically and solve problems creatively in order to become masters in it. When I was doing my degree project, one of my professors told me that I should try to do everything by myself so that I could feel unconditional love and excitement for the research work. Creating a syllabus in this manner during the learning process provides you with the best practise of your passion. You progress to mastery. Hello Master!

2.3. Sexy learning

We live in the age of artificial intelligence. We have numerous opportunities to learn everything. Furthermore, the AI age provides us with more distraction opportunities. We live in both the best and the most dangerous epoch in human history. People who overcome distractions become part of tomorrow's history. I am a person who, like most people, has a lazy mind, is easily distracted, and has a fear of doing things. But I decided to push through and began exploring myself. Because discipline is crucial during the learning stage. When I think of discipline, I remember someone telling me as a child, "Try to learn from school; once you finish school, college life will be very nice and free." When I went to diploma college, where I expected to have fun, people told me to focus on the next two years and your work life will be happy. When I first started working, people told me that I couldn't expect to have fun because I had to learn new things every day, work a lot, and take care of my family. I was perplexed because my family needed money to repay the loans and interest. I used to meditate in the morning, just sitting and thinking about what I had missed to analyse and experience in the past, and what I was missing now. I told myself to enjoy each and every moment as the days passed, but I tried everything to be happy. Nothing, not social media, not outings, not chatting, gives me an image of myself. When people in my department were speaking one day, I felt compelled to explain dimensions because I had previously seen a YouTube video on the subject. At the time, one of my co-workers asked me to share that video, which I will explain to you tomorrow. Could you guess that I couldn't speak in front of people despite being a good speaker in college? I wanted to know why. I don't have an answer. Another day, when I couldn't answer a simple question, my senior said, "Hey, you're in the R&D department, you should be very clear in all the technical terms, but you don't even know the basics, what are you?" I was afraid of myself for some reason; all the images I had explored inside myself in diploma college were gone. Why, I questioned? Why, why, why? I finally got the answer, that I stopped learning. I realised how important every-day-learning is. Then I went back in time and examined everything, people in my past who were mentors, teachers, and everyone else who had led me down the wrong path. Every day's learnings must be enjoyable for me. Because learning is my true mean. I must have enjoyed learning every day in the past, present and also in future. Every stage of myself will be happy if I realise that I have to enjoy learning. You know what, I can also manage my work life with happiness, because when I learn a lot, I can make more progress in my work. However, instead of being promoted at work, I was forced to resign my job. Life driven me to make this decision, and because I wanted to improve my knowledge, I ran away from my company. As a diploma candidate, I am restricted to advance, which means I am unable to investigate more difficult problems in the company where served. So, I resolved to learn and pursue my passion. I went to university, broke down all the barriers within me, graduated, and started my first aerospace business while still in college. Starting a business is not difficult; anyone can do it; however, having a fearless mindset and being committed to continuous learning is essential, a big deal. Money is another factor. But, you know, once I realised that learning is important for life, I began to enjoy every moment of my life, and I began to look for a way to achieve financial independence. In a year, I launched several businesses. But we must understand one thing very clearly: learning should be everywhere. Not just on topics of interest to us. We should be aware of everything that is going on in our lives. We should notice and learn from everything, whether we are conversing, waiting for the bus, talking to a child, giving a public speech, or making mistakes. You know what, someone who realises that life is a learning experience should live in the present moment becomes very disciplined. Every person with a high level of knowledge is disciplined. This is why those people exist; discipline leads to learning, and learning leads to success.

You have the question, Maha! How does one become disciplined? How did you become a disciplined individual? In the beginning, I couldn't devote enough time to any activity other than the one that piqued my interest. In this regard, many people associate with my character. I need to make money; I can't afford to waste my time. What would I do, after all, I was born as a human, right? But my desire is enormous. So, I decided to make myself productive by learning how to spend my free time productively. How should I schedule my learning and relaxation time to make progress in my learning stage? I devised the sexiest method of learning that provides me with knowledge as well as process time with relaxations. I discovered what things can help me relax. I tried reading books, scrolling through social media, and so on. I eventually found my way. This is how I spend my productive relaxation time. First, I figure out what makes me happy and peaceful in my mind. I enjoy chocolate and ice cream. I enjoy both pets and simply sitting. So, as shown in the image below, I planned my learning time.

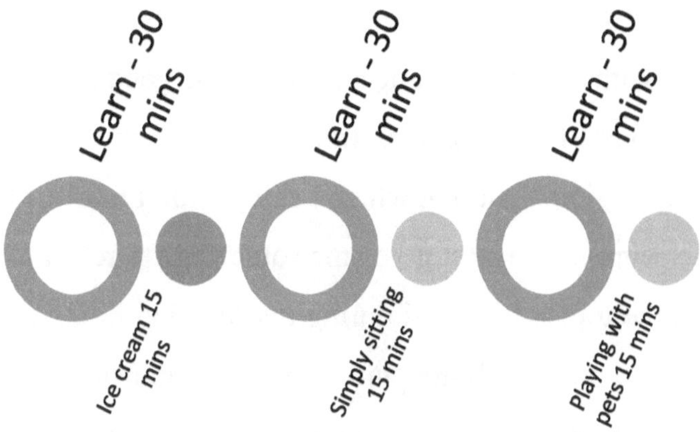

Here you can see that how I spent my time in very productive manner. Again, I can hear something, oh it is your mind voice "Is this a productive way?" Yes, my dear friend. This is a very productive way for me to live my life while I am learning. I spent 30 minutes learning and 15 minutes relaxing by eating an ice cream; eating ice cream gives me energy and refreshment. When I return to work after eating ice cream, I have the same energy I had when I awoke in the morning. Playing with pets is essential for pet development. So, I decided to schedule playing time in between my learning process, which will provide me with relaxation while also providing good care for my pets. Two outcomes from a single action. Then there's simply sitting, which I enjoy a lot. I mostly sit to relax. Because it gives me some time to recall all of the topics I learned during my learning time, and sometimes my brain will generate some new and simple ideas to solve my most difficult problem. Every day, I follow this cycle; I have created a perfect learning period in my life. You can see why I said this is a very productive way for me to spend my free time now. In a nutshell, you should relax your mind after a lengthy learning process by engaging in productive activities. Productive action in the sense that the time spent on these actions should improve your learning ability rather than consume your learning time. For example, if you choose to scroll through social media, you may spend an hour doing so without realising it. So, when it comes to scheduling your learning process, use caution.

2.4. Learn – Earn – Learn

You are now on the right track of learning. However, you may require financial assistance, as I did while in the learning stage. I am a person who wishes to relieve my parents of the torments of debt. Loan/debt is the most torturous thing in the world. But I am grateful for the loan because it lit a fire in my mind. But, at the same time, I want to start earning money as soon as possible because my parents are mentally dying and I'm still learning. I was perplexed as to what I should do. You know, I tried part-time jobs, trading, and freelancing. Nothing provided me with the ideal method of learning and earning. We can see a lot of engineers in India delivering food and earning very little money despite putting in a lot of time, effort, and energy. I was the same way. You know me; I'm the type of person who can't keep doing the same thing if it's not interesting. As a result, nothing had a significant impact on my learning and earning. Also, those part-time jobs took up a lot of my time, which hampered my learning. I see that most young people make this mistake. They will not look inside themselves; they have become a machine, and the energy they expend to do the work is money. We must have a clear understanding of what we are doing. When we work, we should focus on both learning and earning, not just the money. If your job only provides you with money, you will fail in the long run. It will have an impact on your learning, concentration, and mindset toward success. But, thanks to me, I discovered the issue with learning and earning at the same time. I forced myself to plan the goal's flow path. My ambition is to establish an aerospace industry. I need to constantly improve my knowledge in order to become a master of aerospace engineering. If I do useless part-time jobs like delivering food, data entry, typing, and so on, those will not provide knowledge and will have an impact on my learning process. Because I need to work at least 5-6 hours per day to earn a decent living. But I couldn't devote 5-6 hours a day to a pointless job. So,

I decide to look for a job that is closely related to my goal. I tried several approaches; it is an aerospace industry, so we cannot get a paid internship just like that, and opportunities are scarce. But I eventually found a way. I made the syllabus so that people could learn, right? I developed a live online course in the aerospace industry based on that syllabus. But keep in mind that I'm still a beginner. I began receiving registrations for my live online course. Guess what, I made money before I started learning. As a beginner, I felt so good that I made money even before I created the course. Then, in the morning, I studied the topic that I had listed in my day one syllabus, and in the evening, I taught live classes to my students. I carried on with this process throughout the learning process. I became a master at the end of the live course, and I now have a way to make money and a business. That is how I built my online educational business. At this time, I'd like to thank everyone on my team who is working on this. It would not have happened without them. I called the strategy LEL - Learn Earn Learn.

This strategy allowed me to expand my business while also making me the master of my goal. You should know that I built two businesses using this strategy. One is the aerospace industry, and the other is the online education business. And, most importantly, I did not spend a single penny on my businesses. The beauty is that I made money to help my parents and to develop my product for my aerospace company.

"Successful business starts with ***ZERO***"

PHASE 3

MINDSET

3
PHASE MINDSET

Hello, Master. You are now earning money and have mastered your passion. That's fantastic, my friend. I'm overjoyed that you've reached PHASE 3. And I have to express my appreciation to you because you are still travelling with me. Thank you very much, my friend. In this PHASE 3, you will discover your inner leader. Are you prepared? Greetings and welcome to PHASE 3 - Mindset.

3.1. The Born

As I've always said, I represent the majority of people in the world. You can see people who look like me all over the place; perhaps that is you. That is the primary reason I am writing this book. My childhood ambition was to be the leader of my group. I attempted to become a class leader. But in order to be a leader in the classroom, I must in first place. As you are aware, I am a typical student. I never figured out how to learn when I was a kid. So, because I was impressed by movies, I aspired to be a good sports player. But I was certain that even if I were to take another birth in this world, I would be unable to participate in sports. That's how I'm so bad at sports. So, I decided to participate in other activities. But the heck is I couldn't speak in front of a group of people. Wherever I go, I become a member of a group. To be noticed, we should speak precisely and clearly. When you are noticed by the people, you will be given the opportunity to become a leader. But I couldn't say a single word in class because I'm an introvert, a very shy person, and mentally easily broken. This is how I grew up until I reached high school. If you want to be a leader or achieve in your career, being in a higher authority position is very important. You can go higher authority position when you start learning, speaking, and helping others. People used to tell you in school that you should become a higher authority figure, such as a big doctor, scientist, or business owner. You believe that once you have completed your studies and begun to advance your career, people will begin to dump you into a group of people by saying myths about higher authority such as higher authority makes you stressed, higher authority requires high potential ability so you can't, higher authority requires recommendation, higher authority takes time, higher authority requires experience, simple life will give you happiness, higher authority will separate you from your family. But the reality is that no one is going to dump you like this until you've messed up someone else's business. For example, to understand the power of higher authority, I spoke with a professor who lives in the middle class and has worked for almost 24 years but still does not have a good laptop to do his work. He told me that I finished my Ph.D. in six years, but what was the conclusion? I am still earning less than 30000 INR per month. But you are unique, Maha, because you decided to start your own business. To complete a master's or doctoral degree, you must devote at least 5 years and spend at least 10 lakhs. Instead of spending lakhs and years on degrees, you can easily build an industry within that time and money, giving you a great life style. Not only him, but the majority of the people I've met in my life have been supportive and encouraging. You will not face any negative motivations from them unless you disturb their business. People who are attempting to follow their dreams will look up to you as an inspiration. We live in the age of the internet, so no one has time to dump you. The irony is that they don't even have time to look you in the eyes. That is how people in this world are getting faster. The issue is that we are seeing social media posts, movies, and comic books. The majority of the content in these things actually gives you the impression that you will be dumped by people as you grow. But most emphatically not. "Hey Maha, you might be missed to see my life, people here aren't encouraging me," you can say. They're dumping me to the ground. "How much do you know about me?" I agree with you, my friend; people are dumping you. However, you must thoroughly investigate that scenario.

> *"Confidence and hard work are the best medicine to kill the disease called failure. It will make you successful person"*
>
> *-Dr. A. P. J. Abdul Kalam*

Why are people abandoning you? You are simply integrating two or more things, which is why you feel this way. For instance, every member of the lower and middle classes may find themselves in this situation at some point in their lives. When I decided to resign from my job and pursue a university degree, my father asked his brother for help in paying my admission fee. His brother remarked, "Why is your son resigning from his job, he is a fool?" He'll never get another chance like this again. He was never paid this much again. What's more, my starting salary is 13,500 INR. Do you believe it is sufficient to live in this world in 2019? But my father's brother, who earns a lakh per month, wanted to make his son a doctor. He is making more money and wants to improve his son's life. However, when they enter the lives of others, they become demotivating. That is not their fault; it is ours. See, my father asked him for help, which means he is getting into his brother's business, and his brother began dumping us. Isn't it our mistake? If we had chosen a more straightforward route to admission, I could have avoided this demotivation, right?

Another instance is one of the major events in my life. My mother borrowed money from various people to run the business. However, she failed to manage the money; by paying the interest, she forced herself to take a profit and capital amount in order to repay the interest money. She now has no capital to continue the business. The sum was substantial for a middle-class family. I and my mother were surrounded by nearly ten people who were scolding my mother and my entire family. They accused us of being liars because we failed to pay the interest money. However, they increased the interest rate; she used the entire borrowed amount to pay the interest to them. But they were accusing us of being liars. You can't imagine being in that situation, where you're almost as old as me and your mother is mentally dying. They took everything from us, jewels, bike, car, everything. They were full of negative motivations and bad scolding. Consider the following scenario. We went back to zero. Nobody, or very few, will survive this situation. I don't have the opportunity to live my life. But I chose to live, to face the most difficult period of my life. I was born again at that time. I asked for more time and assured them that I would repay the entire amount. They stated that you are unable to repay the borrowed funds. You are going to die because you lack knowledge.

> *"Never stop fighting until you arrive at your destroyed place – That is, the unique you. Have an aim in life, continuously acquire knowledge, work hard, and have the perseverance to realize the great life"*
>
> *-Dr. A. P. J. Abdul Kalam*

They humiliated me, destroyed me, and laughed at me. If I included this issue in my goal, I might lose my motivation to succeed or die at this time. I remained silent, not saying a single word; I simply requested them for time to repay very calmly and kindly after deciding to face this phase of my life. Guys, I'm here now. Have a clear understanding of my life, both are different, they don't even know what I'm doing, what my abilities are, and so on. But they were saying that we couldn't trust you because you couldn't repay the money. Have a clear understanding of the situation; as I previously stated, I disturbed their business by failing to repay their money. That is why they are discouraging me.

So, no one is going to dump you until we mesh with their business. So don't make a fool of yourself. Be wise and clear-headed, analyse everything, and nourish yourself with good things. All of these events got me thinking, "Who am I?" What am I supposed to do with my life? What exactly can I do? What does my birth signify? Why am I here? After analysing all of these situations, I came up with a goal, a desire, I improved myself, I trained myself to overcome the challenges, I broke down all of my barriers, I increased my guts, I became kind, I became unstoppable, I made myself a leader, and I am training others to be leaders. Finally, I was born as a leader for the second time in this world. I am not a head weight in this situation. I'm just revealing who I am right now. And the beauty is that my parents only gave me my second birth. Haha…

3.2. Big is a big

"Only big can make big"

Having a big one is easy when you are ready to do the big one. Confused? Continue reading to learn the distinction between having a big one and doing a big one, as well as what a big one is. --- You may have heard that if you want to go higher, you should do big things. For example, in business, choose a higher-level business; in studies, choose a high-rated course; and in employment, choose a high-paying job. Everyone tells you to go for the big one everywhere you go. Even if you need assistance, people will advise you to contact a prominent figure in your community. Take anything, people need a big one, and they inspire you to get one. The people are ruled by "Big." That is, the term "Big" has become an important part of our lives, careers, and everything else.

So, I have a question for you: everyone tells you to pick a big one and be a big one. But how many people have that big one in everything and always tell you to pick the big one? How many people are there? Could it be 1 or 2? Sometimes the answer is no one. Do you understand why? My friend, the only reason is fear. But people will never accept it; instead, they will complain to others. For example, suppose one person is going to an interview for the position of HR manager. But he couldn't get through the interview.

"The interviewer has no sense to ask questions, he is asking me unnecessary questions that are not required for this job," he will say. That person who went to the interview for the HR manager position did not even try to explore himself. They want the big one but will not try to get it. I had a funny experience in my life when I was interviewing a female candidate for the position of HR Co-ordinator at my company. I was given the opportunity to ask one question about children in order to assess her team-leading abilities. To start the interview, I asked her one question: "Do you like children?" She replied, "No, I'm not looking for a relationship or a child right now; I'm focused on my career." WHAT!!! I was stunned. (This is my reaction.) Most of the people are here in this manner. I also had a funny moment with another female candidate. It's a problem to ask such a question. So, I tried another approach. As I told her, she should think of me as a team member. I gave her the task of leading me without pushing me to achieve a goal; she should be friendly and approach me in a friendly manner to make me do the job. Could you guess what her next move will be? Okay, Sir, first you do, and then I will do the same. "Hey, you have a beautiful red icon at the bottom of the screen, click that button, and you will have silence, give it a try," I said. Examine how people use their abilities. Not only these two people, but I have had numerous similar experiences. They want big one, but they're not going to try to do big one. Everyone in the world wants to get a big one. Big in terms of salary, job, authority, prize, gifts, recognitions, and so on. But the question is, do they go big? You can ask me what it means to do something big, because I'm learning and working harder than ever. See, my friend, wherever you go in any field, everyone is learning and working harder. But what distinguishes you from them? Why do you deserve a big? The difference is demonstrating that you are truly committed to doing the big thing. We have, for example, one of the world's best cinematographers, Roger Deakins. He is putting in the same amount of effort and energy in cinematography as others. Then explain why he is regarded as the best cinematographer and why others are not. Because Roger Deakins knows where he needs to work in order to show his work in a big way. His work provided a significant amount of value. There are so many entrepreneurs here, so how did Elon Musk become so famous? He is a regular person who works just as hard as everyone else. Because he knows where he should work in order to make his work big. For example, in his learning stage, an app developer explored everything about app

"We are all born with a divine fire in us. Our efforts should be to give wings to this fire and fill world with the glow of its goodness"

-Dr. A. P. J. Abdul Kalam

development, from market research to the final output, including architecture, front end and back-end development. When he goes to the interview, the interviewer will also ask him questions about everything related to app development in order to assess his skill. But when he gets to work, he will only do one thing for the long run. That is, instead of using his full potential, he is increasing his time and energy to compensate. I recall Cristiano Ronaldo saying, "Talent without work has no meaning." Similarly, retaining full potential and working extremely hard has no meaning. The majority of people behave in this manner. Despite their talent, they work for others rather than for themselves. As a result, they only add low value to their work. So, wherever you go, try to explore yourself by realising your full potential. If you don't get the chance, don't be afraid to switch platforms. Nothing is riskier than not realising one's full potential.

Some may doubt, "Should I work for myself and not for others?" As a result, Am I need to start my own business? Starting your own business is highly encouraged. I always tell my friends, students, and team members that they should start a business and that I will support them. But, in this case, I mean that you can start your own business, work in any company, but you must still work for yourself. You must discover yourself. Self-awareness is essential for success. What you do is not a thing; what you create is a thing. Another example is that people are constantly building and renovating houses and offices. As a result, carpenters are in high demand. But why are most carpenters paid so little? Because they are putting in the effort and time to create something small rather than something large. This is because they only benefit one person. Consider a carpenter who hires a group of carpenters and covers the entire town to provide his services to everyone in his town. In this regard, he is now providing enormous value, making and getting big. He is putting in the same amount of time and effort, but he is making a lot more money.

I told you a while ago that I left the top company because I couldn't develop my skills there. In fact, I was deteriorating there. I decided to quit my job and travel to a location where I could explore myself and obtain a root map to get to my destination. While family is necessary for financial support, leaving a job is not an easy task, is it? But I resigned from my job. I'm not saying that you shouldn't consider your family situations, where you are in your life, and your family, or that you should quit your job if you don't like it. Not everyone leads the same life. Perhaps the problem they are facing is similar, but their lives are not. Some may face it, while others may succumb to it. So, be cautious when making a decision. Because your decision will have an impact on everyone who is dependent on you. But, I believe, you can find a better place to realise your full potential and explore yourself in order to add significant value to your work. I used to tell my team, "Explore yourself!" You get the big one when you use your full potential in your work and create a lot of value. My friend, Make a big!

3.3. One day or day One

> *"Man needs difficulties in life because they are necessary to enjoy the success"*
>
> *-Dr. A. P. J. Abdul Kalam*

Procrastination, my friend, was a big deal in my life. I had to work hard to overcome my procrastination at work. There are numerous scientific reasons for procrastination. I don't know anything about procrastination from a scientific standpoint. But after analysing myself, I discovered why I always procrastinate. My first realisation is that I value my sleep more. Second, I enjoy watching movies. Third, I did not place a premium on work quality. These three factors seem to be the most common among those who procrastinate. Some people also procrastinate because they are uninterested in the task at hand. But I hope you understand, we only have to do the job or business that we are passionate about and are well-versed in.

People who are interested in their jobs will not procrastinate due to a lack of interest. Even if they are interested, they will procrastinate for various reasons. I tried to overcome procrastination, but I made the mistake of removing the things that cause me to procrastinate. Because sleep and enjoyment are critical components of human life. We can't even move forward with proper mental strength without these things. You should know that during my learning stage, I could work nonstop for three to four days. I lost my mental health conditions, you know. I became sluggish and stressed. I couldn't sleep at the proper time. Late nights and early mornings ruined my entire productivity. That's when I realised how important sleep is. So I resolved to get a good night's sleep. But I'm not sure how many hours of sleep I need. After many trials, I discovered that I require eight hours of sleep per day. Isn't that a huge? You may recall that many successful people sleep three to five hours per day. But you know what, I realised, it doesn't matter how many hours we cut; what matters is how early we start our days and how productively we plan our days. So don't feel bad if you needed 8 hours of sleep. I made a schedule in which I decided to go to bed at 10 p.m. and wake up at 5 a.m. I know I only have 7 hours of sleep when I need 8. I do, however, meditate. So, I guess giving up one hour isn't a big deal for me. It also has no effect on my health because I use meditation to compensate for the one hour of sleep loss. I have time to do all of my activities after 7 a.m. every day. I used my sexiest learning strategy to keep me interested in the learning process. And I do other things like go to college or work, eat, and so on. I fall asleep quickly after finishing all of my work. If I do not maintain a healthy routine, I may become tired while learning, and starting to learn causes me to sleep. Sleep causes me to miss work.

Second, I enjoy watching movies. Before we begin, I'd like to make one point very clear to you. Most parents chastise you for not watching the movie. Still, I see a lot of kids who are forced to stop watch movies in order to focus on their studies. They actually yearn for some downtime. Actually, the film isn't that bad. People loved watching live drama contests in the 1960s, but by the 1980s and 1990s, they had switched to watching movies. I don't mean that movies make people addicted to them or that we spend our money to watch them. The entertainment has actually become a productive approach. Single time video graphing will give the life time watch opportunity to everyone. If the contest is still live, people must travel to the venue or wait in line for a long time to watch it. As a result, I see entertainment platforms transformed into a time-saving productive approach. But keep in mind that we now have OTT platforms where we can watch multiple international films at any time. It provides access. This is where people squander their time. When we finish the first film, there will be a suggestion for the next similar film. It entices us to watch another. This one more will be followed by several mores. The same issue I've had in the past. So, I set a challenge for myself. I set a movie as a reward for myself; if I finish the work, I will receive this reward. Every Saturday evening, I get a reward. This motivates me to complete the work quickly. But understand one thing: we all want to enjoy life, to enjoy each and every moment by visiting different countries, places, and cultures by achieving financial freedom. So, I don't think enjoyment will have no effect on our process if it is limited.

The final factor is producing poor quality work. You know what I had this problem with because of the reward I set for finishing my work. Yes, I agree that it motivates me to finish the work on time. If I didn't finish the work on time, I forced myself to do it poorly. Isn't it a major issue? Working for a while but producing poor results is not acceptable. It is completely useless. Of course, every method has disadvantages. Similarly, my strategy had a disadvantage. You know what, I devised a simple trick to persuade myself to do a better job. I just created a reward strategy for completing tasks with higher quality. Because when we perform well, we reach the pinnacle of happiness. Because it results in dopamine segregation. You already know that I have a strategy for working productively, so why do I need a reward for that? So I decided to give myself a prize if I finished the work perfectly. I no longer procrastinate.

"One day or day one"

I told you I sold chicken biryani on the side of the road. I was afraid and embarrassed to have a roadside shop with only one table and chair. You know, at the time, I didn't have any plans to make money quickly. My mother is an inspiration to me because she made a promise to herself to repay the loan. I was taken aback by my mother's bravery. She is 46 years old, she has lost everything, but she is still willing to work hard and repay the loan in a responsible manner. But she has no idea where to go. But I know the way because I adore my mother's cooking. I always tell my mother that she should open a restaurant. She didn't do it. But life forced her to do it later. I recommended my mother by explaining everything I knew about selling food. How much we can earn, and how to proceed properly in order to make a good profit in this business. But there was one blunder. We were embarrassed to sell food while standing on the side of the road. We were procrastinating by looking for alternatives. We were thinking about starting soon. We were all waiting for that day to come. Look at how stupid we are. When the day arrives, we must make it a day to day one of work. My mother and I both failed. But it is my cousin who is always behind my success, who is always taking care of me and my family, who is always a part of all the ups and downs in my life. He turned that one day into day one. When we awoke, he approached us and said, "We don't have time, we need to start earning right away, or we will lose this life." So, he told my mother to start cooking, and he said, "I'll go sell all the food on the roadside for you." He completed day one. That really opened my eyes. Why should we feel guilty about selling food on the side of the road? We started cooking, went on the road, sold the food, and made a 50% profit on the capital amount. My mother discovered a way to make money from her hobby. She is a 45-year-old woman who discovered her interest and knowledge and began working happily at this age. That is why I say no matter your age. If you are unhappy with your job. Find out what interests and knowledge you have and pursue it. I can see that the majority of people who have reached the age of 30 are dissatisfied with their jobs. They have a lot of responsibility to complete as soon as possible at this age. People should be required to provide for their families. Each and every person bears the responsibility of providing for their family. That is the primary reason they put off doing what they enjoy

> *"Never give up on your dream no matter how old you are no matter where you are today, do not give up dreaming for a better tomorrow"*
>
> *-Dr. A. P. J. Abdul Kalam*

and want to do. But, I argue, we don't have to quit our jobs to pursue your interests. Alternatively, you can change your job to one that is more relevant to you. If you want to start a business while working for someone else, no need to be concerned; in this age of the internet, we have plenty of opportunities to implement the best business strategies. There is only one thing we need to change in our lives. Our mindset, “We can't do what we want while we're caught up in another action". It's incorrect, in my opinion. It is completely incorrect. See, when I insisted on my mother cooking a chicken biryani for the roadside shop, I managed all three of my businesses at the same time. I work for my aerospace company in the morning, sell chicken biryani in the afternoon, and work for my online educational company in the evening. We can do a variety of things together. You are aware that I claim to be the world's laziest, average, and shy person. But I shattered everything. If I can do it, then anyone in the world can. You must make a decision, my friend. One day or one day!

3.4. Attitude makes or kills

"What we show is not an attitude

How we face is an attitude."

It's amusing to remember my adolescent mindset. At the time, I believed that our attitude is how we display ourselves to society. For example, don't respect anyone, walk like a jerk, raise your voice, or speak sarcastically. But then I realised what an attitude was. I literally became a disciple of Lord Buddha. A lot of kids are like me when I was a teen, right? They thought they were matured because they walked, spoke, and treated others with attitude. However, they appear to be children in my opinion.

Let me use myself as an example: When do I show attitude? Isn't it true that when I feel like everything is just below me? People who are in a higher position than others understand that they are only in a higher position of authority or financial wealth, not in a higher position to rule over others. People who are unable to make themselves financially independent, who are unable to manage their lives properly, and who are unable to think wisely, act as if they are the boss. Despite knowing all of this, they continue to act as if they are in charge. Consider the first question: When do I show attitude? I stated that the feelings I am experiencing are just below me. But the question is, why should I believe that everyone is beneath me? The only explanation is an inferiority complex. No one will put me down, no one will treat me like a slave, no one will dump me, but I still feel inferior in front of everyone. You know what, there is no reason for this inferiority within me. That is complete overthinking about the character of others. Judging others, being envious of other people's lifestyles He couldn't live that way; he doesn't know how. As a matter of fact, he begins to imitate them. For example, a small boy sees a king who commands all respect, who orders others, who awards prizes to others, who dresses, speaks, and walks like a top one. He will act like a king in front of his gang, assuming all of the characteristics of a king. He'll be impersonating a king, right? People who are unable to obtain that position begin to imitate the wealthy. But unfortunately, no rich person will behave in the way that ordinary people believe. Rich people understand how they got rich and where they started.

My mother used to say to me all the time, "Who are you? What brings you here? What do you require? "Never forget where you came from." These phrases were created to remind me of my journey to desire. These phrases remind me of who I am. These phrases made me realise that I am not the greatest thing. I remember who I am whenever I recall my starting point. I can relate to everyone. Everyone appears to be equal in my opinion. Some argue that the past is the past. Don't waste time thinking about the past in the present. Don't waste your time worrying about the future. Live in the present. You're being duped by those people. We gain head weight by forgetting the past. Failure results from acting without a plan. Please be wise, my friend; the past gives you the present.

> *"You cannot change your future, but you can change your habits, and surely your habits will change your future"*
>
> *-Dr. A. P. J. Abdul Kalam*

The present determines the future. I agree with the expression "live in the moment." However, living in the present without understanding who you are and what you want to be is not an effective way to live. It will only provide you with content for social media scrolls. Give the life experience only if you know who you are. What's more, successful people never say "live in the moment." "Find out who you are," they'll say. All of these things altered my perspective on attitude. I realised that our attitude is not what we are displaying to others. An attitude is how we face ourselves. An attitude determines how we approach problems. Everything we do is influenced by our attitude. It is an attitude that determines how we inspire others. It is an attitude that determines how we support others. An attitude determines how we guide others. When you realise what an attitude is, you become more kind, polite, and humble. You know what makes you the king, the leader? Attitude. But, to be clear, being a leader does not imply having authority over others. It forces you to collaborate with others. When you understand what an attitude is, it makes you powerful, it makes you think, it gives you importance to your words, it gives you the motivation to work hard, and it makes you unstoppable. Real attitude makes!

3.5. With great power comes great responsibility

With great power comes great responsibility, the famous dialog from one of my super heroes' films. As I previously stated, attitude gives you power, makes you think, and makes you unstoppable. All of this means that when you figure out what attitude is, you become a leader. When I was younger and yearned for leadership, I assumed that leaders had superior work skills and a killer attitude. That is how I grew along with my thoughts as a result of the influence of this society. I couldn't make myself a leader, you know.

> *"Be active, Take on responsibility. Work on things you believe in. If you do not, you are surrendering your fate to others"*
>
> *-Dr. A. P. J. Abdul Kalam*

When I realised what an attitude is, I transformed myself, sculpted myself, groomed myself, and rose to the position of leader. Is that enough to become a leader, you might ask? Yes, it is sufficient. However, as you explore what is an attitude, you will discover ways to overcome your fear, problem, and find the path to the destination. You know what, you can't stop yourself from helping others who are similar to you. Attitude transforms you into a God-like being. Some may misinterpret the term "God" in this context. The term God here refers to a helping character, a supporting mentality, a growing together mentality, and a mindset that treats all people equally. I'm not saying you'll be given more authority to command everyone. Instead, being a normal person with a genuine attitude is the only way to achieve all of the above God's characters, which I stated is unavoidable. You become a leader regardless of how many people you support. It is a question of whether you are assisting the people. When you advance in hierarchy, you have a greater responsibility to look after others. Following everything I said in this book makes no sense unless you have a genuine attitude. However, when you have a genuine attitude, you will succeed. For example, if you want to start a business, you must provide people with employment opportunities. When you have a genuine attitude, you will not treat them as a boss. You present yourself to them as a leader. You will do everything you can to help them succeed. These qualities of a genuine attitude person made me a good leader and brought me a good team. They are happy when we team up, grow, and explore together. When you accept the responsibility to care for others, the number of people you care for does not decrease. It will rise on a daily basis. Even if you are try to reduce the number, your attitude will not allow you to stop supporting the people. When you start taking care of more people, your responsibilities will grow as well.

"When go higher you explore yourself better, when you explore yourself better, you go higher".

That is, when you help a larger number of people, you gain n-number of life experiences. Every day, you will learn something new about yourself. The main point is that we cannot assign numerical values to our characteristics. People say that to be a leader, you must have the power of words, learn to coordinate others, and learn to motivate others.

In reality, you are confining yourself to leadership characteristics. We cannot limit a leader's quality or positive characteristics. Every day, life teaches you something new about helping others. Every day, you discover yourself in yourself. Every day, you remember who you are and why you are here. Every day, your vision improves. When it comes to positions of greater responsibility, you can explore yourself indefinitely. When you explore yourself infinitely, you go as higher responsible person infinitely. Those who understand the above principle, becomes a history, a pioneer. We have a lot of great people in our history who explored themselves and helped others to explore themselves.

3.6. My life principles

I'm not saying you have to live by these principles. But adhering to these principles has made me who I am today. I am a person close to you who began a journey to the desire and is now gone. There are numerous self-help books available; everything will teach you valuable life lessons. But nothing will happen in your life because most people have failed to correlate with their circumstances. To summarise, not everyone is dealing with the same life issues. So, obviously, their tricks and strategies will not work for you. But why are people reading them, and how are they succeeding in life? Because they understand how to formulate in accordance with their circumstances. They succeed! My friend, we have arrived at the end of our journey. I believe you explored different phases of your life during this journey. My friend, be consistent. Every day of our lives, we should only do one thing. Explore! Explore, explore, explore! Every event teaches us something. When you eat at a restaurant, the server will teach you the lesson of hiding your pain. If you are travelling, a travel guide will show you the importance of engaging with nature. If you're a student, a guy will teach you how to communicate with others. If you are a businessman, an employee will show you the way. If you are a teacher, students will show you how to teach. Are you a book author; everyone will demonstrate the lesson of behaviour. If you have a boyfriend/girlfriend, your partner will teach you a lesson in support. If you have a sibling, your sibling will teach you the value of great care. If you are a son or daughter, your parent will demonstrate the lesson of desire. If you are a father or mother, your child will demonstrate a life lesson. Every moment, we learn and explore from anyone we come across. Explore!

My life changing principles are here for you,

"Attitude is everything, but first find out what is attitude."

"What we show is not an attitude, how we face is an attitude."

"Struggles in life inevitable. Gone through it make life compatible."

"Learn everything in non-sense, learn from everything is a sense."

"Be silent while being shame, disrespect, bully. Quite is not bad than quit."

"Think, sort, analyse and do."

"Do big make big."

"Time is dying every second. You can't repay it without your success."

"We get chance again after every single failure with the lesson."

"Don't try to love what you do. Try to do what you love."

"Leadership is not about making people follow your path. It is about making people progress in their path."

"There may have been some dark moon in your life or may come in future. But if you have passed it, the world will admire you like a full moon."

"Loan sucks you."

"Uniqueness is not in how show ourselves. It is in how we sculpt ourselves."

"Don't waste time by looking for the luck."

"Don't wait to do what do you want to do."

"Consistency is a key."

Author' Message

Well, I'm not a person who knows everything. But I am the person who knows how to know everything, and I tried different methods until I found the simplest way to know everything. I shared various strategies that I tried and succeeded with at varying phases of my entrepreneurship journey. You are aware that I am a part of the world's major category. I see a lot of people who live similarly to me. Everyone, including myself, is constantly striving to achieve something. But they couldn't find a way because of time constraints, responsibilities, financial constraints, or their mental state. The truth is that I, too, have experienced all of these causes in my life. I swelled into the financial crash volcano, I lived among very poisonous people, I wasted my time, I got fucked by my mind, and I lived as a completely useless person. But I overcame everything. You know everything right now, your interest, knowledge level, money making, and mindset. So, I'm not going to give you advice right now; instead, I'm just going to tell you that "if I can do it, then anyone can." Just go ahead and do it right now!

I'd like to express my gratitude to you, my friend, who is on his way to becoming the best entrepreneur. Enter to Preneur!

ENTER TO PRENEUR

Change your Interest to Business

BY MAHA VIGNESH N

www.ingramcontent.com/pod-product-compliance
Lightning Source LLC
Chambersburg PA
CBHW050019170726
48282CB00025B/465
9789357797917